Douglas Knocks Out Tyson

Poems inspired by
blood, sweat, spectacle and sentiment

Robert Eugene Rubino

UnCollected Press

Cover Art:

Raphael Rubino
Static Electricity
8"x10" acrylic on canvas

Back Cover Portrait:

Jay Solmonson
Portrait of The Author
San Rafael, CA, 1972

Book Design by:

UnCollected Press
8320 Main Street, 2nd Floor
Ellicott City, MD 21043

For more books by UnCollected Press:
www.therawartreview.com

First Edition 2022
ISBN: 979-8-9867243-2-4

Table of Contents

In memoriam

For Gene and Jo

One Night Under the Tokyo Dome
(February 11, 1990: Ode to James 'Buster' Douglas)

And down goes Buster
like a 231-pound 6-foot-4 side of beef
hitting the slaughterhouse floor
courtesy of one whale of a wallop from Mike Tyson.

And that figures
since the experts made Buster a 42-1 underdog
with an emphasis on dog
the experts smirking while explaining
Buster doesn't have the heart — never has never will —
for this brutal badass bloodsport.

So of course it figures ...
after shocking the world for seven rounds
looking like the second coming
of Cassius Clay against Sonny Liston
Buster making Iron Mike look rusty
Buster bigger stronger faster
Buster beating Iron Mike to the punch again and again until ...

Down goes Buster in Round 8
like a big bad drunk thrown out of a bar at closing time
landing with a ring-rattling thud hard on his ass
from one perfect explosive right uppercut
Iron Mike reaching down deep for some spare dynamite
down deep for some righteous true grit of his own
as if he were the second coming of Jack Dempsey.

Sure, Buster beats the ref's long lazy count
— but barely — up at the count of nine
he looks out on his feet saved by the bell.

Of course it figures ... couldn't be otherwise:
often flat sometimes good never great James Douglas
beating unbeatable wunderkind Mike Tyson?
James Douglas graduating from chump to champ?

1

— Only in your dreams, Buster …

But on this night under the Tokyo Dome
Buster is a man on a mission
to make his dream come true just this once upon a time
and so he resumes his Cassius Clay impersonation
— supremely skillful and wide-eyed willful
turning Iron Mike into One-Eyed Mike in Round 9
… and then … in Round 10 …

James Buster Douglas of Columbus Ohio KO's Tyson
with left-right combinations
right out of a mythical textbook co-authored by
Jack Johnson-Joe Louis-Rocky Marciano
Tyson counted out while on his hands and knees
— a bully merely mortal rendered pathetic
mouthpiece hanging out of his mouth like a pacifier askew
— James Buster Douglas ascending becoming
heavyweight champion of the world.

It's Buster's night his one and only night
this night under the Tokyo Dome once upon a time
and there'll never be another — nothing close to it.

But no need for another … no need at all.
When you have a night like Buster had under the Tokyo Dome
when all the preparation & perspiration pay off so perfectly
when your recently deceased mother
and your child's seriously ill mother
combine to provide once-in-a-lifetime invincible inspiration
all you need is that one night once upon a time
to soothe your aches & pains your cuts & bruises
to ease somewhat your inevitable decline
through all the cheerless rounds of life still to come
all you need is that one night once upon a time
to comfort and nourish you through all the nights all the years
through all the jabs hooks crosses low blows & sucker punches
through all the cheerless rounds of life still to come
… still to come.

Uncool Kid

Were you at Shea Stadium in 1964
when you were sixteen
when you were living right there in Queens
when the Beatles
made their historic histrionic U.S.A. debut?

Yes, you were at Shea in '64! Yes you were!
... but it was to see the Mets-Giants Memorial Day
doubleheader with your dad
and the second game lasted twenty-three innings
— more than seven hours
and you & your dad stayed for all of it!
Loved all of it!
Never got bored
not for a minute.
Never thought of leaving
not for a second.
Loved all of it.
Every run-hit-error of it.
Loved all of it!
Every crowd-thinning seat upgrade of it.
Every hot-dog eatin'
soda-pop slurpin'
Cracker Jack munching
peanut shell spittin' bit of it!

People said it wasn't as cool
As seeing the Beatles.
They still say it.
You said it was way cooler than the Beatles.

And ... You still say it.

Was that heaven?
No. It was just father & son
spending all day all night watching ballgames in Queens in 1964
bonding like nothing else quite could ... or ever did ...

Was that heaven?
Well, it sure as hell wasn't Iowa.
Yeah, that was heaven!

DiMaggio

To his baseball public
there was no actual person
no real flesh & blood & bones
as fucked up as anyone
— lonely, shy, sly, suspicious, driven
terrified of poverty
fearful of failure —
in 1936 no real air-breathing heir
to Ruth & Gehrig
underneath those pinstripes
no complicated human being
thrust into superficial superstardom at 21
he was just Joltin' Joe —
stereotyped as the strong-silent
moody Mediterranean type
his stature defined not by
his smarts or sensitivity
but by sensational statistics
his praises sung loud & long
— Joltin' Joe DiMaggio we want you on our side.

Sportswriters who were frustrated real writers
called him the Yankee Clipper
… as if he were a born-to-the-manor
New England country-club WASP
or a sturdy sailing ship out of a Melville novel.

The Big *Dago* or the Big *Wop*
is what his own teammates & managers
called him — and not just behind
his first-generation Italian-American back
upon which he carried them to glory
season after season
even as the FBI threatened
his illiterate non-English speaking
immigrant fisherman father back in the Bay Area
with detention in a wartime camp.

5

The Big *Dago*. The Big *Wop*.
It was meant in fun, they say,
in camaraderie
but in the dugout during games
he chain-smoked cigarettes
& gulped black coffee
alone — alone among teammates.

It was a different time,
a less sensitive time, they say
— political correctness
as unheard of
as dark-skinned ballplayers playing ball
for the celebrated New York Yankees
as unthinkable as
an African-American U.S. president
as unlikely as
an all-American sports hero
with that non-American-hero-sounding name:
DiMaggio.

Do-Overs
(And So What If It's Some Sixty Years Later?)

This time …
making father-pleasing game-winning catch & throw
instead of cringe-inducing game-losing error
on Little League's rock-strewn sandlot
within noggin-gnashing noise of LaGuardia's
arrivals & departures … its greetings & farewells.

This time …
hitting nothing but net — *swish!* —
instead of hitting just plain nothing
with mind-of-their-own air balls
at junior varsity tryout
in jocks-socks-sweat-smell gymnasium.

This time …
emoting lines — thundering lines —
booming with clarity and gravity
like a pale Paul Robeson
instead of stuttering stammering
in school play plagued by tongue-tied stage fright.

This time …
standing up to the playground bully
instead of bowing head
backing down
peered at pitied like lab slab specimen
by the whole world it seemed …

— including innocent idolizing kid brother
— including first-ever girlfriend
kid brother's hero-worship souring like expired milk
first-ever girlfriend soon to become first ex-girlfriend.

This time?
This time …
things will be different very different …

7

do-over different.
Oh, yeah. Oh, yeah.

Ode to Floyd Patterson (1935-2006)

You got knocked down twenty-two times,
which might be ok for a punch-drunk palooka.
Thing is, you got up every time.
Ok, *almost* every time. And often got up and won.
You were no palooka.
Inspiration to bullied boys everywhere, that's what you were.
Highly skilled fighter, that's what you were —
fast fists, fleet feet, leaping left hook and peek-a-boo defense.

At 21, youngest to become heavyweight champion of the world,
knocking out old man Archie Moore, the legendary Mongoose.
First to regain the title, prevailing over Johansson
in thrilling trilogy.
You might've been robbed of improbable third title
but no complaints, blame game beneath you,
and that, too, an inspiration.

Despite distinguished career spanning three decades,
you're lost in boxing history's fading footnotes,
maybe because your reign so quickly got overshadowed,
nearly erased, by self-acclaimed upper-case
Greatest of All Time;
or maybe because you had a hell of a tough act to follow,
Marciano — the undefeated, undisputed real-life Rocky,
who might've been merely lower-case greatest of all-time.

Your decency rang as clear and true as an opening-round bell,
humble in triumph, conciliatory toward fallen foes.
Humiliated in defeat, you donned disguises
that failed to cover soul-shaking shame
after Liston KO'd you in the first round. Twice.
As two-time former champ, you answered Ali's
slick sadism with misguided masochism. Twice.

You marched with MLK, met with JFK,
and in emerging era of amplified trash-talking gibber-jabber,
you honored your much-maligned sport,

9

respected all fighters at all times,
held your dignity high and your profile low,
unplugged, under the radioactive bombast. Unbowed.
Victory Over Myself — a curious title for your autobiography.
Genuine nice guy in bad-ass racket. Genuine gentleman.
Which is to say: a gentle man. Which is to say: Manly, truly.

Nor Was He The Marlboro Man

They were at Yankee Stadium
father & son
to celebrate the son turning thirteen
at Yankee Stadium not to see the Yankees
but to see the football Giants
which is what New Yorkers still called those Giants
to distinguish them from the baseball Giants
even though the baseball Giants had abandoned New York
for San Francisco three long seasons ago.

They were at Yankee Stadium
father & son
to see the football Giants — *their* Giants
the son disappointed, crushed really,
to learn Conerly — *his* Conerly
nursing an injury from the previous week's heroics
wouldn't quarterback the team this day

— the father secretly joyous shamefully jealous of Conerly
with whom he shared a birth year but nothing else
nothing a teenage son would find heroic.
Unlike Conerly
the father wasn't the Giants quarterback
nor was he the Marlboro Man.

They were at Yankee Stadium
father & son
the father sad, shocked really, to see Gifford — *his* Gifford
tackled so cruelly so violently
Gifford's blue helmeted head bouncing
like a dribbled basketball on the street-tough turf
the vision of Gifford's beautiful body carried off on a stretcher
providing a blinding flashback to luckless friends at Luzon
fifteen short years earlier

— the son shamefully secretly jealous
of Gifford's toughness & courage & movie-star looks

11

jealous of Gifford's gridiron grace Gifford's ability to inspire
awe & admiration & actual cheerleader cheers & tears
from the father
— nothing a scrawny awkward
buck-toothed bookworm teenager
could ever hope to inspire.

Wrestling vs. Boxing

It's false, it's fake, it's fantasy, it's scripted, it's silliness
and at 14 I can't look away.
Musclebound bound-for-glory Bruno Sammartino
getting set to pin villainous Killer Kowalski to the mat,
golden-maned Nature Boy Buddy Rogers
sneaking up from behind and clobbering Bruno
with a folding chair, cueing 601-pound Haystack Calhoun
to come to the rescue.
A magnificent melee ensues while the see-no-evil referee
becomes an incurious bystander.

In my pliable Play-Doh of a mind, pro rasslin'
via our 12-inch black-and-white TV in 1962
was violence stylized, violence operatic,
violence as theater of the absurd
with ample amounts of huffing and puffing
and blowing the house down
with headlocks and dropkicks and body slams and back-breakers
and skull crushers and sleeper holds.
Violence at its best because nobody got hurt
— they'd all be back next week — good as new.

Of course the attraction was made stronger by the revulsion
expressed by my blue-collar father
— well-muscled himself — whose bellowing "It's phony, it's
staged!" cued my cry of resistance:
"Oh yeah? Mr. America's bashed head bled last week. Real
blood!" — even though I knew
it's all fake, even the blood, but that wasn't the point, the point
being we watched stuff together while eating thick-crust pizza —
my rasslin' on Thursday nights, his Friday night fights.

I'd soak up his punchy boxing history lectures
 about the Great John L. and Gentleman Jim
and the Jacks — Johnson and Dempsey
and Joe Louis, of course, while mesmerized by
the sweet-science artistry of aging Sugar Ray Robinson

or one-eyed courage of Carmen Basilio
but neither of us was prepared for the finale
in the Emile Griffith vs. Benny 'Kid' Paret trilogy,
Griffith beating Paret to death
after Paret called Griffith *maricón*
earlier that day at the weigh-in.

Griffith punching Paret in the head twenty-five times
in the twelfth round,
Paret giving nothing in return, Paret slumping
but still on his feet, the ropes holding him up
but he's already gone, gone to where a K.O.'s black lights
never blink, past the point of no return
while referee Ruby Goldstein stares at this public execution
as if he's merely a curious bystander.
It's true, it's serious, it's unscripted, it's brutality, it's reality
and at 14 I can't look away.

Catawampus

When you're the one who leaves
you're a conscience-scrubbed surgeon (or cold-blooded butcher)
you're calm & capable running a complete con
you're a self-serving peace-loving war monger
when you're the one who leaves
you're a smug bonfire-building book-burning thug
muddying memories, rewriting history
fierce savage destructive
you're Employee of the Month at Orwell's Ministry of Truth
when you're the one who leaves
you rip out the rear-view mirror
you stomp on the accelerator
you're a regular bat out of hell
infamy incarnate *persona non grata*
when you're the one who leaves.

When you're the one who's been left
you're left lonely angry anemic
unable to grip cold hard truth
only righteous regret
self-respect so suspect
there's no food no sleep no break
from pathetic plunge
into all-day all-night pity parties
when you're the one who's been left
it's devastating enervating humiliating
it's earthquake tornado volcano fiasco
you're askew awry victim chump uncool fool
when you're the one who's been left
you're cast in rejected roles in surreal scenes
of grand opera comic opera (but mostly) soap opera.

The Hawk Who Became a Phoenix
(Ode to Connie Hawkins, 1942-2017)

Before Michael Jordan staked out his own rarefied air
defying friends and foes and Isaac Newton alike,

before Julius Erving as Dr. J floated above the fray
of elbows whipping around like machetes in fields of sugarcane,

before David Thompson earned the nickname Skywalker
for above-the-rim better-than-sci-fi special effects,

before a firmly grounded peach (basket) of a game
dramatically changed in attitude & altitude

there lived a swooping soaring scoring playground legend
as none before — Connie Hawkins a.k.a. the Hawk.

But instead of gliding to stardom, the Hawk found only exile,
first from college for fixing games he never fixed
— no evidence, no witnesses —
then from the NBA by its prejudiced pious pooh-bahs,
the Hawk was forced for years to fly in small-time skies
or be locked in the gilded cage of clownish Globetrotting.

Finally getting his day in court
finally playing on a big-time home court
symbolically enough in Phoenix
where his career rose from ashes,
an older wiser Connie Hawkins a.k.a. the Hawk
swooped and soared and scored his way to all-star acclaim
and beyond into immortality
— or at least the Basketball Hall of Fame.

Idled Iceless Shark

Perhaps he's a pandemic-idled iceless Shark
— that masked bare-chested thick-black-hair-flowing
young teeth-missing muscled man roller-blading
down ghost-town Palo Alto's Middlefield Road
holding hockey stick in his gloved hands so thick
pushing bad-luck puck of season's sudden isolation.

Perhaps he's a pandemic-idled iceless Shark
from down the road in nearby San Jose
where once rowdy raucous lively arena
now stands as spooky scary silent
as probing prowling Pacific predator.

Perhaps he's a pandemic-idled iceless Shark
daydreaming goon role of slashing tripping or high-sticking
vile viral villain numbered 19 named Covid.
Or perhaps he's a pandemic-idled iceless Shark merely
daydreaming slap-shot goals & Stanley Cup champagne.

Gym Rats of Silicon Valley

Those who sit at the biceps curl machine
the only thing curling their lower lips
as they stare dumb at smart phone screens
reading news or weather or sports scores
or texting (*Hey, 'sup? Just sittin' here at the biceps machine ...*)
or whatever they're doing while not curling their biceps
oblivious of anyone patiently or not-so patiently waiting
indifferent to common courtesy and general gym rule:
Don't Hog Equipment! as they set phones aside
to concentrate on yet another set of bicep curls
(or leg extensions or chest expansions or
back and shoulder whatevers)
as if they're Schwarzenegger at Gold's circa 1975
concentrating on winning yet another Mr. Olympia title
when most likely they're merely
GoogleFacebookTwitterTeslaStanfordHooverInstitue
Yahoos.

Duel at the 'Stick
(July 2-3, 1963: Ode to Spahn vs. Marichal)

They were like classic Old West rival gunslingers
one a grizzled nice-guy cold-blooded killer
with a reputation built nearly 20 years
and spanning the continent
the other a relatively fresh-faced newcomer
— a dandy — not yet famous
outside his small Dominican domain or Candlestick Park
— his big-league home on the shores of San Francisco Bay.

They were like classic Old West rival gunslingers
except they didn't pack six-shooters
instead they pitched fastballs curves sliders
change-ups & screwballs
with variations on each and variations on each variation
baffling opposing batters making the best of them look as foolish
as drunks swinging toothpicks at mosquitoes.

Instead of gunslingers maybe they were
more like symphony conductors
the way they controlled the rhythms of a game
the way they dictated who did what on the field and when
but maybe they were more like Renaissance painters
creating baroque masterworks using palettes
as brightly and brilliantly varied as a Golden Gate sunset.

Each displayed high-kick windups the equal of any chorus line
but their similarities ended there
one coming out of white working class Buffalo
earning a World War II Purple Heart
before ever earning his first big-league win
now the winningest left-hander in baseball history

the other a black Latino right-hander
off his family's fatherless Caribbean farm
bravely navigating the mainland's double barriers
of skin color and language

already with a no-hitter and World Series experience
but several truly illustrious seasons of his career still ahead.

And so in front of a sparse night-game crowd they dueled
a runner thrown out at home in the fourth
a would-be-home run missing by inches in the ninth
neither team scoring inning after inning neither pitcher blinking
dueling beyond the ninth beyond the twelfth beyond the fifteenth
And then in a crack-of-the-bat instant ...

thirty-one minutes past midnight in the bottom of the 16th
Willie Mays (of course — who else would it be?)
slew the old-man gunslinger-maestro-artist-pitcher
with one shot one shot into the dark and fog of the 'Stick
into its nearly vacant left-field bleachers into the dark and fog
of time and memories ... of record books and trivia.

Postgame Wrap

He's the kind of person who …
after a selfish-selfless inner tug of war
gives her his prized well-insulated
San Francisco Giants windbreaker
because he's got another windbreaker
(no team logo but just as good)
and she's got none and they'll be sitting
in the bleachers and it likely will get cold & windy
around the seventh-inning stretch
even colder and windier on the postgame walk
about a mile long along the Embarcadero
from the ballpark to the Larkspur ferry.

She's the kind of person
who gives her recently received
well-insulated Giants windbreaker
to the shivering sleeveless homeless man
she sees curled up like a fetus
along the Embarcadero
during their postgame walk
from the ballpark to the Larkspur ferry
— the kind of person
who does such a thing instinctively
not thinking nor caring
about her own privileged comfort.

He's the kind of person
who clutches awkwardly at annoyance
and stubborn shameless resentment
like a bratty hyperactive child
at the Monterey Bay Aquarium
trying to grab hold of an eel.

She's the kind of person
who has as much use
for resentment and annoyance
as that eel does — the kind of person

who follows her big-hearted impulses …
and never looks back.

Stickball Hallucinations, 1958

Narrow parked-car-crowded silent sauna streets
tamed under Idlewild's cacophonous summer skies
became the wide-open cheer-splashed spaces
of old Yankee Stadium a borough away in the Bronx.

Sawed-off broomstick in your bony hands
became thin-handled big-barreled Louisville Slugger
& ten-year-old skinny scrawny zero you
became Superman in pinstripes No. 7 muscular Mickey Mantle.

Spaldeen pink rubber ball innocently savagely struck
became official big-league hard-as-granite hardball
its red-stitched white horsehide streaking like a comet's tail
into the upper deck's facade of cream-scalloped crowns.

Vanity Unfair

Chapter 1: Childhood

Too small, too weak, too shy,
too ... well ... childish,
believing in Santa & Jesus
& Pledge of Allegiance
& professional rasslin 'on TV
far too much for far too long.

Chapter 2: Adolescence

Teeth full of braces, face full of zits,
plump, pointy, puss-filled pizza-face zits.
Too skinny, too tall, too lazy, too cowardly
to fend off bullies, to express sexuality.
Too conflicted, too, attracted to
philosophies of the pope & Playboy magazine

Chapter 3: Adulthood

Able to pass for normal at last,
future is now, what's past is past.
Teeth straight, complexion clear, muscles toned,
weight in sync with height,
shyness out, hedonism in, sexuality expressed
alas and alack, careless and faithless.

Chapter 4: Golden years and beyond

Bald scalp, blurred vision,
turkey neck, prune face,
achy hips, slower streams of piss,
arteries hardening, erections softening,
heartburn, heartache,
irritable bowel, irritable soul.

Epilogue

Oh vanity so foul, oh vanity unfair
and still whining after all these years.

Starr-Crossed

You smoke the dope of horoscope
got the same January birthday as Bart Starr
winning quarterback in the first two Super Bowls
but back then you were a passionate fan
of the upstart league of Broadway Joe & Oakland's Mad Bomber
you hated
the stuffy NFL
your father's NFL
with its pitilessly perfect Packers
you hated
'winning isn't everything it's the only thing' —
Lombardi's right-wing wrong-headed
muddled mantra.

They Weren't Playing Polo at the Polo Grounds
(Ode to the 1954 World Series)

... tied in the eighth, Liddle pitching, Wertz batting,
crowd quiet as if in outdoor cathedral praying,
underdog Giants World Series hosting
Cleveland team of record-breaking Yankee-killing
beneath Coogan's Bluff next to Harlem River flowing,
at the Polo Grounds where polo's never playing.

Wertz connecting sounds like musket firing,
Wondrous Willie in centerfield turning, hustling,
Wertz's ball majestically soaring arcing,
into wild green yonder Say Hey sprinting,
Ruthian fly falling to Earth after 460 feet flying,
No. 24 back-to-home over-the-shoulder catching.

In extra inning Lemon pitching, Rhodes pinch-hitting,
fungo fly flies mere 265 feet landing
in grandstand's not-so-grand overhanging
at the Polo Grounds where polo's never playing,
anywhere else Rhodes' can o' corn not game-ending,
but it's the Polo Grounds where polo's never playing.

Visiting Cleveland in for stunning sweeping,
while back home hard by Lake Erie soon reeking,
Cleveland faithful in for generations of grieving.
Anyone else but Mays in center it's an alternate ending,
Anywhere else Wertz would've been heroic for homering,
but it's at the Polo Grounds where polo's never playing.

Sonny Liston Workshops His Creative Nonfiction in the Hereafter

Phantom punch my ass and no pit-a-pat punch neither. Three times in first-round rematch Clay hit me with rights right upside my head and third time I never seen it comin' and I go down— hey that shit happens. Then that fool stand over me hollerin' and cockin' his fist like some prison punk like he never heard of no neutral corner, sportsmanship, respect for the other fighter. I say why get up just then just so he can hit me upside my head again? And him standin' over me like that — that become a famous photo and people look at it — they still lookin' at it more than fifty years later — like he some kind of bad-ass hero.

And don't get me goin' about Jersey Joe — good fighter, ex-champ, nice man but good-for-nothin' horseshit referee. He leave Clay standin' over me, go over and jaws with itty-bitty timekeeper. Meanwhile, Clay finally step back, I stand up and we start mixin' it up again and then I'm fucked — Jersey Joe come back to the action, says I been counted out even though nobody done no countin' that anybody hears, least of all him. He raise Clay hand say Clay he still be heavyweight champ, which make me heavyweight chump. Fans and press and even other fighters — every soul on Earth 'cept my wife say I took a dive. Well, Elijah's scary-ass FBI-infiltrated Muslims just done kill Malcolm and that shit do make me think.

You know what else make me think? How people believe what they want to believe. How people don't like facts gettin' in the way of what they like to believe, what they told to believe. Like how people think Clay served prison time for standin' up to the man. Hey, it's cool he stand up to the man by not lettin' the army draft his ass, but his pretty face never spent a day locked up and that's the truth. Me, they throw me in the Missouri State Penitentiary, motherfucker. Stand up to the man?
The man teaches 12-year-old Clay to box.
I stick the man in a trash can and take the man's gun and badge.
So who be the real bad ass?

But phantom punch my ass and no pit-a-pat punch neither. That
clown Clay he too quick too slick (just like first fight) and he hit
me upside the head — never seen it comin'. But after that I got
no shame bein' second-best fighter in whole motherfuckin'
world for next five years till I die — still don't know what went
down that day. Think by now I'd been told. But no.

Word here in the Hereafter say maybe he and me get it on
for fight number three. If it comes it comes.
I got nowhere else to be. I'm already in tip-top afterlife shape
and word 'round here say Clay — ok, I'll call him Ali —
he ain't nearly as fast as he used to be.

Best Friends and Devoted Lovers

In the beginning
so many red flags
it could've been May Day in Moscow:
His guilt, her exes, her guilt, his exes
her snoring, his jealousy, his sneering, her jealousy
her depression, his impatience
her son, his daughter, her dog, his cat
the bottle-a-night wine drinking
& their pretty-pretty-good-but-something's-missing sex.

In the beginning
could they see all those flags
through the shimmering spectacle
through the raw red-blooded blizzard
of all those flags?

Of course they did but they saw them
not as warnings but as bullfighters' capes
and they'd get high on the adrenaline rush
of flamboyantly twirling one red cape after another
provoking seducing the demonic beasts
confident in each other's ability to stick 'em & slay 'em
slay 'em all, cut off their ears, castrate them.

Or did they see all those red flags
as the fiery bright eternal flames
of their midlife revolutionary romantic parade?
Yippee-hooray for red flags!
Let's wave 'em like crazy, wave the fuck out of them!
Laugh in the flags' red faces until their own faces turned blue.

After all, they called themselves best friends & devoted lovers
and they would transcend the red flags
or so they truly believed
rise above high above all those red flags
with work & play & sobriety & creativity
with hikes in the forests & strolls on the beaches

with warm smiles & belly laughter
including laughter at themselves.

But the years the sneaky sadistic years
taking their damn sweet time
doing their dirty nasty work gradually suddenly
and one day it's indeed May Day
as in "May Day! May Day! May Day!"
Life-or-death cries for rescue or escape
the parades & pageantry over
the *plaza de toros* trashed beyond recognition
the laughter and lovemaking
having given way
to binge drinking and neck-deep debt
furtive pot smoking and pill popping
and a brief affair and a not-so-brief affair
the depression not budging not giving way at all
and the amazing colossal jealousies
and a panic attack leading to a night in the ER
and estrangements from children
who weren't children anymore
and the incredible shrinking empathy
unhappiness relentlessly eroding happiness
like sleeper waves crashing into a moonscape
and it's all desperately needing to be cleared away
like so many tons of confetti
fit for neither compost nor recycling.

No Wonder Cepeda Called Him The Latino Jackie Robinson

Far from home he came not to conquer but to play
his play his work his work his pride his pride his joy
his joy his craft his craft his art his art *beisbol*
his skills vast & voracious — hitting for average & power
running catching throwing — the rare five-tool all-star
six if you count an odd and fearless willingness to get on base
by taking pitches off his shoulders his hips his thighs his ribs.

Far from home far from the Cuban & Negro leagues
in which he thrived Orestes Miñoso arrived
in the American League of post World War II
already with two strikes — black skin & *no hable Ingles* —
the dreaded double minority. The gringo press called him
Minnie but there was nothing mini about him
not his courage not his talent not his crowd-pleasing flair.

Saturnino Orestes Armas Miñoso Arrieta was a Cuban Comet
who blazed a trail for Clemente & Cepeda & Tiant
for Aparicio and Campaneris and Marichal and all those Aloud
for the Tonys — Oliva and Perez and for so many others
no wonder Cepeda called him the Latino Jackie Robinson.
Far from home Miñoso came not to conquer but conquer he did
from 1951-1960 a decade of sustained excitement & excellence

Attesting to Miñoso's stature far from home there stands a statue
outside the home of the White Sox on the Southside of Chicago
where he might've been as beloved as Mikita and Jordan.
And — finally — from the sport he loved the sport he lived
long overdue Hall of Fame recognition arrives
bittersweet in that it comes nearly seven years after his passing.

In his own words,* nearing death & still far from home:
The world didn't break me. I never let the world hurt me.
They used to call me terrible things.
This is what the world is like.
None of it stayed with me.

Never did I let them see it bothered me
even though I was crying inside.
On the outsideI just gave them my smile
my smile all the time.

* from Far From Home by Jose Luis Villegas and Tim Wendel
(published by National Geographic Society, 2008)

"Float like a butterfly, sting like a bee! Rumble, young man, rumble!"
— Cassius Clay (before molding himself into Muhammad Ali) bellowing in unison with court jester/cheerleader Drew Bundini Brown, while training for his first title fight, in 1964.

Rumble, Old Man, Rumble

And now, live! From inside your mind,
seventy years in the making,
the moment of truth. Main event in the evening ... of your life —
The Fight of a Lifetime!

In this corner, from the fabled land
of spirit-nourishing stone-cold sobriety,
wearing spine-straight heart-healthy optimism of believing
 it's not too late to make profound personal change ...

Introducing the late-blooming proverbial overnight success
who arrived on this planet some 26,000 overnights ago,
(stretching *fr* sound as if it were salt-water taffy) ...
Frrrreedom Frrrrom!.

And in this corner, wearing know-it-all cynicism
& dead-eyed Darwinian survival skills,
desultory champ for decades of decadence,
weighing in with chump's usual baggage
of guilt and shame, but also shrewd pluck and dumb luck ...
from deep in the heart of long-buried traumas
(rolling the *r* like Orson Welles channeling P.T. Barnum)
— Frrreeedom To!
 Bell rings. Sounds like Reveille. Or Ravel. Bolero?

Freedom To looms like Harm, in the way.
But Freedom From comes ready
to rock and roll, unafraid knowing he might get hurt,
get knocked on his ass, but he's prepared to get up,
bob and weave, stick and move, rope-a-dope.

Freedom To goes for the KO.
Freedom to steal, cheat, lie, get high, sink low,
fuck around and fuck up.
Freedom From counter-punches
floating like a butterfly stinging like a bee
— formula made famous by Cassius lean and hungry.

Freedom From finds his rhythm free and easy,
freedom from righteous indignation,
from revenge, from anti-social media, from angry haunting pasts,
paranoid daunting futures, from addled consciousness,
from deceit, including especially self-deceit, from self itself.

Freedom To throws slow aimless punches at air hot with rot.
Freedom From digs in, cheers up, hears hoary exhortation
enlivened, enriched, transformed, infused with timely twist:
Rumble, old man, rumble!

Before and After

Your father, before he became your father:
a New York City tenement child of the Great Depression
— a deez-dem-doze kind of guy
a stickball/handball-playing stand-up guy
standing up to neighborhood bullies kind-of-guy
a high school dropout who served
under the corncob-pipe-sucking MacArthur
and saw friends and fellow soldiers blown apart
in the Philippines, saw without benefit
of the megalomaniacal general's mirrored sunglasses.

Your father, before he became your father:
emerging from that so-called Good War
with shrapnel-shrouded vision
valiantly tried to board postwar America's
white working-class prosperity train.

Your father, before he became your father
falling in love with another tenement child of the Depression
your father after becoming your father
remaining in love with her — your mother — for 62 years.

Your father, *after* he became your father:
his Franciscan-like kindness softening
the brattiest brats and beastliest beasts
his Ben Franklin-like common sense
and sense of fair play beating back, usually, bunk and bias
— his own included.

Your father, after he became your father:
Never failed to volunteer for family duty no matter how fraught
and fought for family unity with the steady energy
and undaunted determination of a Matterhorn mountaineer.

Your father, after he became your father:
suddenly shockingly switching
from New Deal Democrat to Reagan Republican

a sucker falling for the Gipper's B-movie masquerade
— a source of not-so-friendly great debates
with you his firstborn who'd long since fled
to the friendly confines of the San Francisco Bay Area.

Your father, long after *you yourself* became a father:
his lifelong ocean-swimming athleticism devolving
into seizures-induced incontinence and immobility ...

a slow-motion decline stretching into seven long years
faced mostly with corny wisecracks ...
and with helpless childlike complaints
sprinkled like bitter drops of inevitability ...
until his sigh of surrender at 93.
Your father.

Yahweh in High School (1961-1965)

I.

We nicknamed him Yahweh
because the celibate young-buck
black-robed principal
of our all-boys Catholic high school
loomed like a crazy-scary-angry
Old Testament deity
whether raging against masturbation
(euphemistically called self-abuse)
or dispensing tough-love law & order
with a fist to the sternum
or knee to the scrotum
or hard-pressed knuckles
to the top of the skull
or ritualistic butt-baring paddling
with a paddle that looked like an oar
from the wreck of the Hesperus.

II.

As we survivors of our all-boys
Catholic high school lock-stepped
to off-key notes of Pomp & Circumstance
and endured a grueling gray graduation day
steeped in pledge-of-allegiance speeches
from our principal nicknamed Yahweh
condemning racial integration & godless communism
while beseeching the divine son's virgin mother,
a round red-faced fussy fusty yellow-vested boy
who for four years absorbed loneliness and laconic innuendo
like a true believing saintly stoic Crusader —
graduated to eternity by stepping off the Queensboro Bridge
— a sound bite of news that an eon before social media
still spread among us his classmates
as swiftly as an abandoned ugly urban lot set ablaze
by careless kids stubbornly striking not-so soggy matches.

Trumpassic Park

Of course you didn't know Trump
when you both grew up simultaneously in Queens
his Queens of money and maids and aggression
and assumed supremacy
your Queens a cockroach-infested three-room apartment
for family of five
but looking back now you know
you knew dime-a-dozen Trump *types*
— cold-blooded attention-grabbing bully dinosaurs
reeking havoc wreaking havoc
whether shoving you off your bike
or throwing your ball onto a nearby roof or simply smacking you
for no reason other than to generate fear and establish dominance
— they were as familiar in the neighborhood
as dog feces on the sidewalk.

Of course now in 2020 you cower
at the memories of those bullies and their *Trumptilian* assaults.
You wonder about your role in them.
Were you an unwitting enabler? A bully magnet?
Does the number of times various bullies preyed upon you
say more about you than them?
Something unflattering? Something shameful?
Does it say it's who *you are* that's … well … *wrong*?
And so who are you? What are you?

When there were no witnesses (hell, even when there were lots)
it was easy to pretend the bullying never happened.
It was a gift this ability to compartmentalize
— move on -— grow up.
Either a gift or a magic trick. Or delusion.
After each victimization you were certain it would be *crazy*
to do anything *but* pretend the bullying never happened.

Of course you didn't knowTrump
when you and he grew up in Queens
but you knew all the Trump types — they were a dime a dozen

and you knew them all — all too well.
And after straitjacketed in shameful silence for decades
those memories of humiliation
those memories of emasculation
only since 2016 have they squirmed loose
hissing like infernal serpents.

Maybe that's coincidence.
Maybe not.

Accident on the L.I.E.

We're just cruising keeping pace
with all those cars ahead on the Long Island Expressway
going 60-70-80 miles per hour
a couple of 22-year-olds
leaving their families' old city
heading toward our newly adopted old city
in a not-that-old forest-green '65 Mustang
in the first hour of a four-hour drive
as the sun sets
on our first Thanksgiving weekend
as a married couple.

Siamese cats in the back in their cages
wailing away another day of traveling discontent.
Wife in the passenger seat already dozing already oblivious.
We're just cruising
keeping pace with all those cars ahead …

When two moments' distractions
two what-might've-been daydreams
slam head-on into each other —
football on the radio
Namath injured? Season ruined? …
and then recalling earlier-in-the-day shock
disguised as friendly surprise
when ex-girlfriend girl-next-door dropped by
just to say hi and bye …

No longer going 60-70-80 …
all those cars ahead stopped instead
the Long Island Expressway
transformed into instant parking lot …
All those cars aren't moving
but still rushing toward us
coming closer-closer-closer
— how's that possible?

Will we die?

Hitting the brakes,
slamming hard pressing down hard on the brakes
needing to stop more than the Mustang
but no matter
those cars ahead still
coming closer-closer-closer ...

Will we die?

Slowing down some but not stopping — no, far from stopping
sudden surreal sound of metal smashing,
glass breaking, steam hissing, steering useless
the whole kaleidoscopic scene
simultaneously fast-forward and slo-mo
it's a movie — no it's real too damn real
veering sliding turning spinning skidding crashing
as if on ice but there's no ice
this Thanksgiving weekend has been unseasonably mild
— one might say deceitfully mild.

Sudden-stop-sudden-silence.

Did we die?

Fact Checker's Notes (1996)

Local rag's four-inch murder-suicide story
with itty-bitty 18-point headline
Two Bodies Found
gets victim's age wrong, misspells first name.
She was 41, not 42.
Wasn't Katherine with "e" in middle,
was Katharine with "a" in middle.
Like Hepburn.
Known as Kate, also like Hepburn.
And equally compelling in roles she played:
youth gymnast,
college art student who adored Toulouse-Lautrec
and Hieronymus Bosch,
morose gut-laughing stoner,
daughter of divorce,
jealous of science brainiac big sister,
pregnant at 17 by 24-year-old formerly platonic boyfriend
who followed her from Boston to Berkeley.

But *Two Bodies Found* has none of that.

Two Bodies Found says Kate worked as a waitress;
but omits her being a film aficionado,
her favorites:
the blissfully naive *King of Hearts*
and *The Servant*, a piece of noir psycho-sexual nastiness.

No mention of pop song she liked to lip sync,
the impossibly ironic *I Can See Clearly Now*.

Or that she devoured Vonnegut's dark humor,
idolized the ballet of both Baryshnikov and Bruce Lee,
delighted in reading aloud *Phantom Toll Booth*
& smelled of tobacco and patchouli and cannabis sativa.

Two Bodies Found says Kate had husband (separated),
two sons (ages 10, 14),

but nothing about newborn girl
she and formerly platonic boyfriend
gave up for adoption.
Mother, daughter met once, 22 years later,
on intense day of hugging, mutual crying.
After that day, solo crying.

Killer's name Marsh, real Whack Job.
Was he 44 or 45? Who cares?
Knew Kate for year, little longer maybe.
That doesn't matter, either.
Not to be found in *Two Bodies Found*,
police say — off the record —
Marsh smoked a cigarette after shooting Kate in the chest, twice,
before lying beside her and shooting himself in the chest. Once.

Whack Job's mother spins it as double suicide
— Romeo & Juliet
or some shit.
It wasn't.

King for a Day

Checkers pieces get reset yet again
it's only a friendly game after all, right?
Right. As if we ever played any game
not wanting to annihilate the other.
He calmly assumes air of dignity

while hunched in a wheelchair
his chin looking like it's attached
to plaid shirt's buttoned top button
his oversized diaper bulging
over coffee-stained red sweatpants

his wrinkle-rutted face
splotched with dried blood
result of nursing-home aide's shave
his breath a labor of longing
watery eyes searching for land

his World War II combat brothers all gone
one just last week, now he's the last
his Josie, wife of 62 years, dead three months
family expects him to follow any day now
family will be wrong — by five years.

He makes yet another unruly triple jump
using whatever damn pieces
moving in whatever damn direction
he damn well pleases, this time adding
a flourishing finishing flick of his wrist

and guttural gargle of a command:
King me!
Well, I know a con job when I see it
or at least I think I do.
Hell, I really have no idea.

I sit and stare, shrug and sigh
no more resetting of pieces.
As time and toil crown my father
his tender tenor rasps & gasps:
Give up, wise guy?

Guido

You're nine or ten years old. Everyone likes Ike.
You're riding your bicycle on a street in your Queens
neighborhood
red-white-and-blue plastic streamers flowing from the handle
grips
the neighborhood covered with wet leaves and broken branches
— the remnants of a wicked late-summer storm itself a remnant
of a hurricane that began near Cuba
roiled its way up the East Coast
causing significant damage in those Southern states
that somehow seem more foreign than Cuba
and finally expiring off New York City's beaches
— Rockaway and Coney Island and all the rest —
no longer a hurricane but one hell of a windy rainstorm
nonetheless.

And with a young boy's imagination
the bike riding in the neighborhood becomes an adventure
the adventure being the twisting turning dodging
of all the broken branches in the street.
And then the reverie gets a rude alarming jolt.

Guido the neighborhood bully
(Or is he simply the neighborhood weirdo?
Or the neighborhood's mysterious man child?)
who's 14 or 15 maybe even 16 or 17
walking on the sidewalk with a stride
simultaneously aimless and predatory.

Guido picks up one of the broken branches that looks like a spear
and he throws it at you or at your bike

and it sticks into the front-wheel spokes
and you somersault over the handlebars like a Ringling Bros.
acrobat
and land on your butt stunned and humiliated but otherwise ok.

No words exchanged. No witnesses.
City streets could be like that sometimes somehow
as lifeless as the Catholic cemetery
where the grandmother you never knew is buried.

You and Guido lock eyes for a fugitive finger-snapping moment
his as empty as the Edsel dealership on the corner.
He resumes his aimless predatory amble
as if nothing happened.
You resume your imaginative bicycle adventure
as if nothing happened.

*   *   *

Now ... sixty-five years later
You wonder what became of Guido.
Did he go into the army? Participate in the My Lai massacre?
Did he become ...
a Fortune 500 CEO?
an off-Broadway Method actor?
a talk radio shock jock?
a Republican congressman?
a Trappist monk?
a Heel on the pro wrestling circuit?

If Guido saw you at 74 today
riding a bike down a branch-strewn street

would he at eighty-something wave
a cheery ironic hello of unlikely recognition?
Would he draw you into a comically serious dialog
about the vagaries of the unwelcome roles
we're assigned at various stages of our lives?

Or would he pick up a branch that looks like a spear
and throw it at you or at your front-wheel spokes?
Would he upend
if not your life
at least your perception of it?

Cherry-Lime Rickeys

Heat waves steamy sticky stinky heat waves
these days cast a haze over me a pall
appalling to feel as lazy
as a can o' corn co-ed slow-pitch softball fly.

No skill no thrill no will
to ride these days' heat waves
in this grumpy grouchy
old man odd-man-out daze.

But when we were kids … ah! …
a lifetime ago when we were ten-year-old kids
when the city's soaring searing summer temps
smacked us in the face tried to place us in choke holds
as parental tempers simmered broiled & boiled …

We didn't care
we didn't have a/c
didn't care
we had instead jittery old-fangled fans
that half-assed shoved hot air around
like two sleepy two-sheets-to-the-wind drunks
reluctantly escorting each other 'round-and-'round
in concentric circles.

In the hot humid humid hot steamy sticky stinky
summer in the city when we were kids
we cared about nothing … nothing but playing
all-day playing — deep into the deepening dusk playing
free — fever-dreamily delightfully free —
from frowning fawning adult supervision …

Playing …
on dirt-and-rock fields carved from empty lots
on asphalt playgrounds
on gooey-tarred streets
on cracked sidewalks
in front of apartment buildings
featuring Fallout Shelter signs
with arrows pointing downward …

Playing playing …
whether with a big group small group
just a few or only two
even by oneself …
and one's gold mind of imagination …

Playing playing playing …
baseball softball stickball
punchball handball stoop-ball box-ball
even something called off-the-wall.

And all that playing would be rewarded
at RoJack's candy store's fountain counter
where we'd spend eleven hard-unearned cents
hearing ice cubes clink
while watching sensuous sinuous squirts of syrups
blasted with bubbly water
drinking those chilly cherry-lime Rickeys
the crystal-clear beads of cold condensation
on the outside of our skinny tall glasses
matching mocking cloudy salty beads of sweat

slowly slowly slinking down slinking down
our uncreased brows our fuzz-less faces.

Wanderers All of Us

I wandered into childhood
alone
among so many other children exactly like me
among none like me
wide-eyed silent obedient
but not without sneaky streaks
of narrow-eyed subversion.

I wandered into adolescence
alone
among so many other adolescents none like me
yet none unlike me
all of us so sure of what was what
none of us with even a clue
our script inscrutable and no improvisation allowed.

I wandered into young adulthood
alone
among so many other young adults scared of nothing
nothing so much as scared to death
of turning into our dying parents
who had done nothing wrong
except be themselves.

I wandered into middle age
alone
among so many others wending through the workaday world
so cocksure confident convinced I was an exception —
I'd never fall victim to that cliche virus called midlife crisis.
Oh how proudly ashamedly self-satisfyingly wrong
I was.

I wandered into retirement's golden oldie moldy years
now become supersonic speedy cloudy days
alone
among so many other boomers burdened by pending vacancies
virility vitality having given notice
these clouds rolling roiling presaging end-times storms
storms that will rage and raze and ravage and cleanse and erase.

The Ninja Turtles Pajamas Gambit

In the family photo, a father not quite 40,
dressed in faded blue jeans and an even further faded silver
softball jersey,
sits at a small kitchen table while holding his six-month-old son
on his lap
and playing chess with his 6-year-old son, who wears Ninja
Turtle pajamas.
The six-month-old maintains an expression of puzzled curiosity,
apparently fascinated by the ornate figures
being moved so deliberately by his father and brother.

The father grins, looking lovingly, admiringly at his older son
who hasn't just learned to play chess but has deep-dived into it,
seduced, perhaps, by its promise of control its promise of
superiority.
Contentment, too, lines the father's face
— a fleeting frozen moment of pure parental pleasure.

In this family photo, the 6-year-old has a look of dagger-sharp
concentration,
his focus would appear scary if it weren't for those Ninja Turtle
pajamas.
He has recently learned beyond how the pieces move
— some straight ahead, some diagonally, some multi-directional.
He now knows something (not a whole lot, of course, but
something)
about strategy, about planning moves ahead,
something about anticipating his opponent's moves.

Such knowledge is bound to beget more knowledge, and more,
and so forth.

Such thirst for this kind of knowledge can be a form of lust.

If one were to look closely at this family photo,
one might be able to see more than laser focus in the 6-year-old's
hazel eyes.
One might see a certain driving hunger,
not just a will to win but a primal-yet-insatiable need.

If one were to possess a crystal ball,
one might see in the 6-year-old's rigid posture,
his confidently aggressive reaching for a chess piece with his
right hand,
his tightly pressed lips,
his refusal to acknowledge his father and little brother,
a refusal to forgive, a stubborn (or addictive) insistence
on maintaining a double estrangement that will drag on,
year after year, decade after decade.

What Are We Really Doing
When We Dance the Thermostatic Tango?

Too cold
too hot
too hot too cold
too cold too hot too cold too hot too cold
one sets it at 62 inside
when it's 82 outside ...
when it's 62 outside
sets it at 82 inside.
Other resets it resets it resets it & resets it at 72
inside
no matter what's what
outside.

It's an indelicate imbalance it's all of a piece
a chance these two take to dance
this temperamental thermostatic tangled tango
this funny sad silly serious minuet
this back-bending limbo
into descending dissent elusive consent
this too hot too cold too cold too hot two-step
so cliff-face steep
so chillingly challenging
to find enough room
to negotiate the just-right room-to-live
temperature.

Should be easy but it's crazy
failing to find
a temperate peace
in the place or places

they share (visible and otherwise)
in the abodes in which they reside
in which neither side abides
in the room they make
in the claims they stake
between them behind them
above and beyond
them.

Random Dylan

She catches him again yet again,
absentmindedly playing with his wedding band
(a skinny circle of white gold squeezed-to-death
between buffed black titanium),
slipping it off his ring finger
using only his thumb of the same hand,
deep-tissue massaging it with said thumb
and its neighborly index finger
and just as dexterously slipping it back on.
And then off again. On, off, on, off.
Like a magician palming a plugged nickel.

He thinks of a line from a Dylan song:
This kind of love I'm so sick of it.

It's nothing, he says.
Just a nervous habit.
Meaningless.
There, see it? Back on.

He thinks of a line from the same Dylan song:
Sometimes the silence can be like thunder.

Just pick a random Dylan, she finally says,
after an eternity-and-a-half
her whispery-husky-voiced words floating
like a peaceful breeze in the war-torn air between them,
returning to earth and landing softly
like the hot-air balloon they had ridden on their honeymoon in
Napa

a million years ago when dragons dozed harmlessly in the rolling
hills
and demons dared not rear their ugly heads from the bay.

Suggesting random Dylan is a familiar olive branch.
They'd listen. They'd marvel.
They'd turn to each other. Smile.
Two-part harmony, a beautiful thing.
And as tough and fragile as a high-desert bloom.

And so he commands: Alexa, play Dylan
and he turns the volume up, way up.
And Alexa
perhaps randomly perhaps not
picks "Lovesick,"
the opening track of *Time Out of Mind* from 1997.

And they hear the raspy nasally declaration:
I'm sick of love; I hear the clock tick.

This "Lovesick" Dylan random? No way. Not to her.
No goddamn way.
To her it's a message and she reacts to that message
with the fury of fire and brimstone
and with the gasping gulping sobbing
of the broken girl she once was and feels like again.

And they hear a line that strikes at the heart.
I'm sick of love; I wish I'd never met you.

It's a random choice, he insists

with the bombastic conviction
of a Revival tent preacher.
Don't blame me. Blame Alexa.
And you haven't even heard the last line yet.
He holds his arms out in front of him
palms up as if meditating or panhandling.

The last line renders all the rest crap.
That's the genius of it.

That last line arrives, like a day-old newspaper.

I'd give anything to be with you.

And then that last line flees
as if from a jailbreak
— a fugitive.

When Meditation Was All The Rage

One minute you're feeling enlightened
meditating with brown-robed beatific bald Buddhist nuns.

Next minute you're feeling frightened
by high-beams flashing horn-honking tailgating pickup.

One minute you follow your breath
inhale exhale release restless random distracting thoughts.

Next minute you're breathless
screaming expletives at the expletive tailgater who can't
expletive hear you.

One minute you notice
the modest monastery's sweet still air suffused with serenity.

Next minute you imagine
tailgater's MAGA hat swear you hear truck growl like a T-rex.

One minute you're grateful
for the monastery's sparseness its safe spotless space sacred.

Next minute you'r resentful
of tailgater's sadistic fun at your expense despite how fast or
slow you go.

One minute you hear
nun speak wisely about how all is transient all attachment
suffering.

Next minute you see

your spiritual f-ing afterglow reduced to f-ing ashes on a two-
lane blacktop.

One minute you're kneeling
knowing there's no past no future only the here-and-now present.

Next minute you're screaming
You want to pass me? Pass me! Fuck me if I'm pulling over!

One minute you're at peace
all is right with the world all are forgiven including you.

Next minute you're at war
in your slowed-to-a-crawl car's interior glow you hold middle-
finger pose.

Whatever happens happens. Namaste.

Golden Retrievals

Now in my seventy-fifth year
still got a good outfielder's arm
so I throw a yellowed slightly scuffed memory
as if it were a slightly scuffed yellow tennis ball
far into the middle distance (or occasionally far beyond)
and my newly adopted spirit animal
this scruffy gimpy grumpy old golden retriever
lopes and limps and gambols after it
and to my astonishment brings back the tennis ball
eventually … although … sometimes …
what's brought back is a different tennis ball
— pink or purple or factory fresh or so chewed-up
it looks like something else entirely
something needing to be put out of its misery maybe
or something determined to defy Darwin and survive unfit.

Sometimes what's brought back
is a different memory
or a memory reimagined
or a memory excavated
from under backyard compost or backcountry mass graves
from under fallen wet-with-rot fall leaves
but longing for renewed leases on life.

Sometimes what's brought back
is neither tennis ball nor memory.
Sometimes my newly adopted spirit animal
this scruffy gimpy grumpy old golden retriever
brings back a colored brightly blood-soaked bird
still breathing but barely.

And sometimes nothing's retrieved nothing at all.
Sometimes my spirit animal
returns with empty jaws and mud-caked paws
wide wild eyes filled to overflow
with incandescent innocence.

Childhood's End (Part I)

What was the first name of your childhood best friend?

If it's before adolescence
when vivid palettes of personality are wet with freshness
and the resonant canvasses celebratory
the answer is Gregory
— smart, sardonic, charismatic
(can a 10-year-old be charismatic?)
Gregory taking you under his wing sixty-five years ago
Gregory Batman on Halloween and you Superman
and at his sibling-sloppy happy home later
you two splitting the night's loot
— candy and coins and cookies and cupcakes
and last season's baseball cards.

Gregory and you at 11 sneaking into Sunnyside Arena
to see pro wrestling
— Bruno Sammartino and Haystack Calhoun and Mr. America.

Gregory taking you with his family camping and hiking
in the wilds of the Hudson Valley
— one whole hour away from the city!
you two talking about the adventure for weeks and months later.

Just shy of 13 Gregory introducing you to FM radio
and MAD magazine
to rock 'n' roll and breakthrough comedy
— wacky Ernie Kovacs and subversive Dick Gregory—
after whom Gregory was named …
or so said your white Irish-Catholic childhood best friend
with a wink.

But after age 13
where was Gregory?
Girlfriend? Boyfriend? Family problems?
Different social circles? As if you had a social circle.
Did something happen? Did nothing happen?
Something always doesn't have to happen, you know.
Just a matter of going separate ways?

You'd see each other from time to time — you and Gregory
and as quick as a dead-bolt click
you'd exchange expressionless nods of recognition
like two long-haul truckers
down-shifting into different directions
although for you … it felt more like gears grinding.

Childhood's End (Part II)

What was the first name of your childhood best friend?

After age 13
when disillusion made dissonant music
like mediocre musicians forever tuning up flea-market
instruments
the answer is Timothy
— overlooked undersized underrated
by teachers, coaches, peers, even his own big brawny family.

Sixty years ago at 13 Timothy placing himself under your wing
and doing it rather insistently
despite your initial reluctance resistance
your fortress of solitude
as impenetrable as an Arctic igloo on New Year's Eve
but soon melting eventually evaporating —
for years the two of you feeling low hiding out getting high
in dank cellars or dim Times Square porno theaters
Timothy latching onto you
always and everywhere or so it seemed
and you getting used to it eventually relying on it
throughout high school even on weekends
even at part-time jobs and dead-end double dates
even looking ahead to the draft
were promises made? — spoken or merely implied? —
that when the time came
the two of you together would join up be men do your duty
neither of you college-bound or politically astute.

And just shy of 18 Timothy taking you to a party
in the East Village

at the loft of a friend of a friend of his sister
you not all that surprised there is no party
just the two of you feeling low getting high
crashing there for the night.
Did something happen? Did nothing happen?
Neither of you talking about it after … not a word.
Just a matter of going separate ways?

By 19 Gregory in college
Without you.
By 19 Timothy in Vietnam
Without you.

Brief Survey of Your Recent Lengthy Visit
to Our Emergency Room

1 — The experience of having a needle-sharp tube inserted into the tiny opening in a part of your body never before the recipient of such attention was …

A — so thoroughly satisfying and life-affirming you wish it hadn't ended after merely eight hours (not counting the additional seven days of "home care").

B — rather unpleasant considering the inserted tube appeared to be both wider than the body-part opening and longer than the body part itself (although we assure you that was an optical illusion).

C — such an intensely tortuous nightmare you'd rather have been eaten alive by the Room 101 rats in Orwell's *1984*.

2 — You found the ER doctors, nurses and other workers to be

A — understaffed and overworked.

B — about as compassionate as prison guards at Attica circa 1971 especially when they left you alone for hours to stew in your own "juices" while they presumably tended to higher-priority tasks, patients and busywork.

C — so warm and cuddly you wanted to take a few home with you, maybe even adopt them — except for the nurse who became increasingly irritated when you failed to heed her oft-repeated command to "RELAX!" while she inserted the too-long too-wide needle-sharp tube into the tiny opening in a part of your body never before the recipient of such attention, or the other nurse who became downright frustrated hours later when once again you failed to heed commands to "RELAX!" this time when yet another too-long too-wide tube was inserted into yet another too-small orifice.

3 — If you were to experience another two-day two-way simultaneous "cloggage," you will ...

A — reclaim your lapsed Catholicism and offer your screaming suffering for the souls in Purgatory.

B — reclaim your lapsed Catholicism and hire an Exorcist to rid your innards of the Demon.

C — call a plumber.

Thank you for taking the time to complete this survey. We promise your answers will remain as anonymous as you were to our dedicated ER personnel.

Poets must seek out and cultivate their contradictions.
— Orson Welles

Seven Pillows of Wisdom
with apologies to T.E. Lawrence

I. Be brutally honest
with yourself about yourself
about your arrogance ignorance pettiness pretentiousness
about your everlasting lusting lazy sniveling selfishness.
Be especially honest
about your history of dishonesty.

II. Protect yourself. Forgive yourself.
You are a precious fragile gemstone
gorgeously fabulously flawed.
You are gloriously flesh and bloody human.
Shower yourself generously
with the bloodless diamonds of nurturing kindness.
Cover yourself
with the ever so soothing aloe of self-esteem
demanding deserving to be treated like a celebrity.
Treat yourself. Celebrate yourself.

III. Find out
who you are
what you are
what you're doing
where you come from
where you're going
stand straight stand tall
take no shit
make no sorry-ass apologies …

IV. except when you've done wrong
when you've caused harm
when you slip up fuck up.
Then … slouch humbly
eyes tearful
voice shaky
head bowed
say sorry
say it again
this time mean it.

V. Set boundaries.
Be your own border patrol
sharp-eyed trigger-fingered.
Guard your boundaries
with vigilant valor.
Enforce your personal law:
No Trespassing
— violators will be subject to arrest and prosecution
and may be fined or imprisoned or both.

VI. Be fully receptive accepting
open loving to others
especially the difficult unlovable others
— no excepting.
Provide aid and comfort
anyways always
or at least regularly
once in a while.
You are here to give to others.

To serve others.
Be
of service.

VII. Treat others
not only not merely
as you wish to be treated
treat others
the way *they* wish to be treated.
Go figure.
Figure it out.

Shooting the Breeze

Pleasant
sitting here looking really looking
at this backyard in full flowery bloom …

Unpleasant
that numbing hum & invasive honk
of mainstream media traffic jams
that torturous cacophony of social media's
unmasked cowards & blowhard haters.

Pleasant
this backyard breeze
as nurturing & nourishing
as an honest-to-goodness hug
between prodigal father & forgiving son …

Unpleasant
these damn tears dammed up
close to bursting behind these bleary eyes
wide weary eyes that — all those yesterdays ago —
briefly beheld future betrayals that is this here-and-now
but blissful blindness proved so awfully seductive.

Pleasant
watching this royally named butterfly
shooting the backyard breeze —
a brightly multi-colored aerial acrobat
living its multilayered life
as if there were no tomorrow …

Unpleasant

as if indeed there were no tomorrow
this frightening tightening in the chest
in that space below the throat above the sternum
as if an imp's in there
screwing around with a screwdriver.

Anxiety attack? *Anxiety attack!?*
Too glorious a summer day
for a fucking anxiety attack.

Our Fourth-Grade Grey Nun Explains Purgatory (1957)

Sister said:
Unless we live a rare and holy life
with much suffering and sacrifice
we aren't going to be saints
and therefore aren't going to go to Heaven
not immediately upon our deaths, anyway.

It saddened me to hear that.

Sister said:
Unless we live a rare and evil life
in which we make the lives of others
especially particularly mightily miserable
we aren't going to be damned to Hell for all eternity, either.

I was relieved to hear that.

Sister said:
However *(and this was a BIG However)*

We are more than likely going to Purgatory
— *ok* — which, Sister said, is exactly like Hell — *oh, not ok* —
full of fire and fury
and crying and screaming
in constant torturous agony without pause …

Well, hell, I didn't like that. Not one bit.

Sister again said However (and this was an even Bigger
However)

Sister said Purgatory isn't forever.

Whew!

Sister said:
Before graduating to Heaven
where we will live sort of like the saints' distant neighbors
the length of time we spend in Purgatory
is based on the amount and severity
of our unconfessed venial sins.

Unconfessed mortal sins, we knew — we're fucked
— oops, just committed a venial sin.

As a nine-year-old, I figured my Purgatory sentence
would be somewhere between a week and a year —
what with my sins of disobeying my parents
or fighting with my younger brothers
or lying about this or that or the other thing
or stealing that Superman comic book from the corner store
where I also stared at the covers of 50-cent paperbacks
like God's Little Acre
with pictures of half-naked women on the covers.

Sister said:
We can choose to offer up any any injustice
any pain any humiliation any suffering whatsoever
endured in this life
for the benefit of the souls in Purgatory
thereby shortening their sentences.

Sister said it's sort of like
putting money in their bank account to lessen their debt.

A classmate smarter than I
asked why we couldn't just offer up our suffering in this life
to shorten our own yet-to-come Purgatory sentences.

Sister said …
That's not how it works, young man
And by the way, such selfish selfish
sinfully selfish thoughts
will only add to your Purgatory sentence.

Hmm. How many of us fourth-graders
felt both vaguely informed and slightly ill?
And more than slightly frightened.
How many of us still had a crush on Sister?
Sister with her fragrances of rose water and mimeograph ink
intoxicating us poor captive souls bound for Purgatory.

We Don't Cry to Keep from Laughing

We enter the world crying … nobody greets this life laughing.
Laughter joins the crying later
and soon we come to prefer laughter.
Of Course. It represents fun — a good time.
Crying represents grief. Pain. Sometimes shame — a bad time.

But we can cry tears of joy
— a most profound expression of emotion. Wouldn't you agree?

There is no laugh of misery … or is there?
Bitterly or sardonically laughing at one's misfortune …
We humans can be so clever that way.

A sense of humor might be the most valuable of all our senses.
But laughter can be wicked,
wielded as a weapon to induce crying in others.
Crying — authentic crying — has no such dark side
No such weaponized side …

We laugh to keep from crying but we don't cry to keep from
laughing.
There is inappropriate laughter …
but crying is so deeply personal …
even when it appears to be inappropriate, it's allowed. Excused.
Usually.

Laughing and crying are like best friends with a lot in common
…
but like best friends … a lot *not* in common.

Laughing and crying are like young lovers
full of passions so intense
they seem better suited for an opera house
rather than your house.

Laughing and crying are like strangers from cultures so different
… whose observations and experiences reveal worlds apart.

Laughing and crying are like mortal enemies
— each threatened by the very existence of the other.

Laughing and crying are twin wonders of the human spirit —
deep within us … deep within us … yet … out of our control
— humbling us while enriching us
with a moment's Relief … a moment's Release.

Half Moon Bay Afternoon

The ocean sounds loud today
louder than usual
different
deep-throated deeper
than either rumble or roar
different
not angry exactly
more like do-or-die determined
like it's the world's biggest baddest
grandest grand-scale spaceship
like it's preparing for takeoff
perhaps having conspired with its sister oceans
to leave this earthly realm
escape this trash-choked death trap
to extricate elevate levitate out of its planetary hips
to catch the solar winds
to fall under the spell of other moons
somewhere else in the limitless elsewhere.

We burn we sweat from the unseen sun
seething from behind an incompetent overcast
that's more like a dung-drab threadbare sieve of a sheet
even the sea breeze minutes ago so cool so chill
now feels like a warm exhausted exhale turned hot.

We walk barefoot on the damp pebbly oatmeal sand
we unskillfully skip flat black stones into soap-suds foam
as if we were children
as if we were innocent
as if we were in another time
another world.

We climb one-hundred-and-one wood-rot steps
past Rip Tide and Sleeper Waves warning signs
back to the trail that'll take us
back to our car that'll take us
back into town
for a Mayan meal
— *poc chuc* —yes!
at Cafe Capistrano
our soles long dry
our appetites whet.

Counterfeit Loner

Shy quiet introverted
keeps to himself
reveres solitude attitude
meditator deep-thinker non-drinker.

Like mute Quasimodo in cathedral bell tower
he cherishes sanctuary — sanctuary of alone time …
as long as
he's not actually alone …

as long as someone else
— lover, parent, adult child, sibling, friend,
colleague, cousin — anyone
(except strangers; no strangers allowed)
as long as someone else
sits somewhere else
in the house, apartment, cabin, condo, bungalow …

or at least as long as someone else
(except strangers; no strangers allowed)
is expected to eventually to show up
so he's not actually alone …

so he can luxuriate
in his reading writing scribble scrabble daydreaming …
because if he were ever actually alone — really alone — alone
alone —
— depressing, debilitating, paralyzing —
Terror!
would grip him by the throat
like the ghost of Albert DeSalvo

and squeeze and squeeze out
peace of mind
and like Eliot's Prufrock
squeeze and squeeze in
prickly panicky loneliness … and not let go.

You see, it's an open secret:
this loner can function fully
for only as long as
he's not actually alone.

Beyond the Pale

Old — Check.
Bald — Check.
White?
Well, yeah, in a general, nebulous, amorphous
racial stereotyping racial categorizing sort of way
… I guess I'm air-quotes "white."

But white is the color of a blank page
and I'm not *that* shade of white
I'm no blank page.

Now I've done my due diligence
I've scanned my kin studied my skin
not a particularly pleasant task
when it's skin that covers old-man bones & old-man innards
old-man skin that's been mostly indoors
under dusty white lights for much of these pandemic years.

But in the quest for absolute accuracy
I've done a thorough investigation
and I've found there's more to white
than meets the whites of my eyes:

Why, there are several subtle shades:
There's beige, cornsilk, floral,
seashell and sea salt.
There's white smoke & white ash
and if you don't know the difference
well, you need to brush up on your fifty shakes of white.

There's ghost white (perfect for Halloween).

86

There's the exotic-sounding *alabastrine*
which I'd love to say fits me
like a custom-made sheep-skin glove
although I'm more tastefully drawn to a form of white
— and this is no joke, this is a real shade,
— hey, I looked it up on the Internet —
called *cosmic latte*.
Oh, yeah, man, far out
& make mine with milky-white soy creamer
and extra foggy-white foam, please.

But this is about accuracy not fantasy.
And so, after hours of close examination
day and night all last week and this week, too …
I'd say …
on good skin days Pale Pink would be as precise
as a puss-white pimple.
Bad skin days: Gotta go with Washed-out Pink
—after all, the washroom mirror doesn't lie.

Average day?
Is Beyond the Unwashed Pale a thing?
Well … it's *my* thing.
Especially … first thing in the morning.

Winter Wind

Painful Truth is an icepick-sharp bitter Arctic blast
suddenly showing up barging in taking over
like a crude uninvited guest at your unwanted surprise party
in that bleakest blindness before daybreak
of another weary wintry morn.

Painful Truth is an icepick-sharp bitter Arctic blast
ripping through your gated community
your hidden home with its slick security systems
its safe-solid walls & doors & ceilings & floors
& thick-as-bricks insulation guaranteed a lifetime to last.

Painful Truth is an icepick-sharp bitter Arctic blast
dismembering your distraction devices disconnecting you
tearing through layer upon thickest warmest layer of clothing
shredding your redacted reveries into shards of undressed
wounds
exposing your native naked self lashed to self-delusion's mast.

Painful Truth is an icepick-sharp bitter Arctic blast
whose sunless shock & shiver will someday finally fade
whose polar power inevitably shall turn tame
rendered mute & moot as you get to work doing what's natural:
shielding & sheltering — rebuilding & recovering:

Recast for a new spring repast.

Acknowledgements

The following poems, some in an altered version, first appeared in the following journals:

Ode to Floyd Patterson in *Gravitas*

Wrestling vs. Boxing, **Seven Pillows of Wisdom** and **Rumble, Old Man, Rumble** in *Cathexis Northwest*

Uncool Kid, The Ninja Turtles Pajamas Gambit, When Meditation Was All The Rage and **Nor Was He The Marlboro Man** in *MacQueen's Quinterly*

Gym Rats of Silicon Valley and **Winter Wind** in The Write Launch

Catawampus, Stickball Hallucinations 1958, Starr Crossed, Yahweh in High School, King for a Day and **Sonny Liston Workshops His Creative Nonfiction in the Hereafter** in *Raw Art Review*

A prose version of **Fact Checker's Notes (1996)** appeared as "Spinning Shame Into Nostalgia" in *Hippocampus*.

Cherry-Lime Rickeys and **Guido** appeared in *Newtown Literary*

Gratitude

I'm grateful for family, friends, fellow writers and editors for their invaluable encouragement through the years, among them: Kenneth and Belinda Rubino, Donald Rubino and Larry Buckman, Tom Goldstein, Rich Mellott, Lowell Cohn, Stacey Swann, Rachel Howard, Donna Talarico, Ruben Quesada, Joshua Rivkin and the No Fear poets (George Lister, JoAnne Tillemans, Rebecca Dougherty, Jennifer Trainor and Michael Wachter) of Stanford Continuing Studies, Samuel Griffin, Sandra Squire Fluck, Clare MacQueen, Mary Pitman Kitch, Henry Stanton, Susan Warren Utley and Savannah Spidalieri, Guy Biederman, Tony Aldarondo, Dan Brady, Nazelah Jameson, Lisa Rosenberg and Sandra Anfang. And of course extra loving gratitude to my wife, Terry Jacobs.

About the Author

Robert Eugene Rubino was born in New York City's Greenwich Village in 1948 and was raised mostly in the East Elmhurst/Jackson Heights sections of Queens, with a three-year sojourn in suburban Long Island. He served in the Air Force from 1966-70, including a year at Thule Air Base in northwest Greenland. After graduating from San Francisco State University with a B.A. in Journalism in 1979, he began a 34-year career with various newspapers, mostly as a copy editor, including more than 27 years at *The Press Democrat* in Santa Rosa, California (during which time it was a *New York Times* Regional Newspaper), where he also contributed Sunday sports columns for 21 years. He published baseball fiction in Elysian Fields Quarterly from 2001-09. He received a Pushcart Prize nomination for creative nonfiction (*Spinning Shame Into Nostalgia*, Hippocampus, November 2016). In 2018, at the age of 70, his first published poem appeared, in *The Esthetic Apostle*. Since then he has published prose and poetry in various online and print literary journals. He lives in Northern California.

Endorsements

Phrases such as "action-packed", "thrill ride" and "full of big laughs" are never used to describe a book of poetry. However, in Robert Eugene Rubino's debut book, all three phrases do apply. Even the title is sensational—Douglas KOs Tyson— and reads like a newspaper sports section headline. Rubino amazes with his big love and historian's knowledge of all things athletic, a sports announcer's fast-and-furious play-by-play delivery and an uproarious humor you don't see coming. From boxing to football to "pro rasslin'" to growing up a working-class "uncool kid" in Queens N.Y.C., it's all here as sure as Douglas KOs Tyson. Literary World, meet Robert Eugene Rubino.
— **Dee Allen, author of Rusty Gallows (Vagabond Press) and Plans (Nomadic Press).**

With fire and wisdom, poignancy and tenderness, Robert Eugene Rubino's poetry in *Douglas KO's Tyson* explores legends and underdogs on big stages and in living rooms, on an expressway and over a checkerboard at a nursing home. Rubino's superb craft, narrative strokes and smooth style have created a powerful collection of poems that illuminate, explore, and touch the heart.
— **Guy Biederman, author of *Nova Nights (Nomadic Press, 2021)***

Robert Eugene Rubino's muscular language, skillful alliteration and fast-pitch phrasing in *Douglas KOs Tyson* offer a front-row seat to the drama of competition, whether big-time boxing or father vs. son checkers. And lines such as "Employee of the Month at Orwell's Ministry of Truth" in his more personal pieces had me re-reading this work of a fine poet.
— **Sandra Anfang, author of *Xylem Highway (*Main Street Rag, 2019)**

www.ingramcontent.com/pod-product-compliance
Lightning Source LLC
Chambersburg PA
CBHW022036090426
42741CB00007B/1089